Postcards from Autism

Postcards from Autism

by

Eileen Coughlin

© 2024 Eileen Coughlin. All rights reserved.
This material may not be reproduced in any form, published,
reprinted, recorded, performed, broadcast,
rewritten, or redistributed without
the explicit permission of Eileen Coughlin.
All such actions are strictly prohibited by law.

Cover design by Shay Culligan
Cover photo by Zetong Li on Pexels
Author photo by Mark Turner

ISBN: 978-1-63980-670-6

Kelsay Books
502 South 1040 East, A-119
American Fork, Utah 84003
Kelsaybooks.com

For my daughter and others on the spectrum along with the parents, partners, family and friends, and all of those who love them. May you find a piece of yourself in these poems.

Acknowledgments

Thank you to the following journals that have published poems that are in this collection:

Awakenings Review: "Your Body as an Escape Room,"
   "Fishhooks," "Just Get Over It," "Through the Looking Glass,"
   "Feeding the Beast"
Door is a Jar: "Searching for Answers"
Literary Mama: "This Love Between Us," "Reading the Signs"

Special thank you to Elizabeth Mason who offered her technical, editorial services, advice, and encouragement on the manuscript. Her support has been invaluable.

Contents

Preface	13
Beginnings	15
Postcard—Laughing Buddha	19
Your Body as an Escape Room	21
This Love Between Us	22
The Eighth Color of the Rainbow	24
The Dance Teacher	26
Postcard—It's a Small, Small World	29
The Vacuum	31
Fishhooks	32
Postcard—Staycation	33
Just Get Over It	35
The House of Barbini	36
Through the Looking Glass	37
What About Me?	39
Postcard—What's the Difference	41
Song of the Paper Doll	43
Postcard—Tigh-Na-Mara	45
Putting the Broken Pieces Together	47

Postcard—Oregon Oceanside	49
Framing the Question	51
Behind My Back	52
Keeping Your Head Down	54
Reading the Signs	55
Op Po Sites	57
Postcard—Cedar Point Park	59
The Photograph	61
Postcard—Sichuan, Ten Years Later	63
It's Not a Picnic	65
Feeding the Beast	66
You Stop	67
Trying to Make Sense	69
Over Parenting	70
Celebrating Everybody	71
No Offense, But . . .	72
Grief	73
What Love Looks Like	74
Watermarks	75
Two Dashes of Bitter	77
Hanging On	78
Postcard—The Vdara	79
The Vow	81
On Trying to Fit In	82
Wake Up—Wake Up—Wake Up	83
Stop Pretending	84

Postcard—Unsettling on the Coast	87
For Give Ness Sake	89
You Pretend Not to Miss Me . . .	90
Taproot	91
Searching for Answers	92
Have It	93

Preface

Poetry, while based on lived experience, is not a literal telling of a story. It is metaphorical and intended to allow the reader to make connections to their own lives. This particular poetry collection focuses on my experiences as a parent who has been enriched and challenged by parenting on the spectrum. I caution the reader about drawing conclusions based on representations in my book or any other single source regarding individuals who are diagnosed on the spectrum. Autism exists on a continuum, it is complex, and often occurs with multiple co-existing features. While there are some common characteristics, each individual has unique strengths.

One final note, my daughter has been supportive of my writing but not involved in the process. The poems are written from my perspective as a poet and a parent—and one who admittedly like most is imperfect. "Postcards from Autism" is an invitation to increase insight, generate interest, elicit emotion, and give rise to conversation. I encourage you as a reader to consider how each of us has an opportunity to open our lives to the experiences of those whose lives are touched by autism. My daughter and I both hope you will engage with the poems in a manner that increases understanding and advocacy for those who are neurodiverse.

Beginnings

1.

February—it arrives in a plain manila envelope.
The formal paper from Jiujiang Children's Hospital.

Attending physician, Dr. Wang Hong Tong.
The description of your head—square.

Excluded from the medical report: dysentery,
ear infections, boils, and bronchial congestion.

The black and white picture hides your exquisite beauty.
Outside, horizontal rain turns umbrellas inside out.

2.

August—the stifling heat of Hong Kong.
I perfect the Chinese shuffle, steps taken in half inches.

Bunched together nudging heels, we hail a taxi
to Kowloon rail station, take a bullet train to Guangzhou.

You are delivered dressed in a Mickey Mouse sundress,
as if you were born in California's Disneyland.

Your head is hanging down, arms and legs floppy.
Dancing feet are unable to find ground.

3.

Authorities check my adoption application.
I check your diaper, for dysentery.

Agents have desk work. There is no downtime.
Officials press your foot into black ink pad.

You babble into a box on the page.
Your print-lines smear.

A physician gives you a cursory glance
and signs a form confirming good health.

4.

In Guangzhou, a woman at the Victory Hotel
steps into the elevator and punches the G button.

She turns, prying—baby boy, or girl?
She tries to put her finger in your diaper.

I mail a black and white postcard
of laughing Buddha back to my office.

The secretary tapes it to the towel dispenser
over the sink. You are still sick.

5.

Back in the United States a technician sticks a needle
in your arm, can't find your vein. He punctures and pivots.

You cry as he pierces your skin. He commands
that I calm you, after three tries I lose my temper.

The test report comes back positive for HIV. I feel faint.
The doctor determines it was a false-positive.

These two words do not belong together.
I stand and lift you up; it is how we began.

Postcard—Laughing Buddha

The Yangtze River floods Jiujiang city. Contaminated water spreads cryptosporidium, dysentery, bronchial infections, boils and thrush. Infants are sick. My child is one of them. It's hot and humid. A sewer stench wafts from the sidewalk grates. I am walking to the White Swan, a world class luxury hotel, where there is a medical clinic. The infirmary is hidden down a hallway off the lobby of waterfalls and high-end jewelry stores. A silent baby is strapped to my chest staring at my forehead. Her hair is standing up straight, the sides unevenly chopped. She is still a stranger to me. The other adoptive parents are sightseeing, buying baby outfits. They stroll the streets snapping pictures. I ask the doctor to pose for a photograph. The empty medicine bottle serves as a souvenir.

Your Body as an Escape Room

At home you are talking to the return air vent asking
where I am, when I will get back. There is no answer.

You bounce your body across the living room floor
heels slamming against the carpet—the first clue.

Lifting one leg at a time you study them in the mirror,
make a mental map, it is how you learn to walk.

You run through the kitchen wiggling your fingers
and shouting phalanges, phalanges, phalanges.

The clock is ticking, I can't fit in your shoes.
There is no space for me. I stay up all night crying.

I prepare a dish of fettuccini, you vomit violently
into every room of the house trying to escape yourself.

Your body betrays, assaults your senses. You resent
years of therapy—scripted to meet pre-defined social skills.

Live every moment as if yesterday never happened.
There is no pattern in your quilt.

But the colors are stunning.

This Love Between Us

Other mothers meet at coffee dates. They share
conversations about crawling and cruising furniture,
chatting and comparing major milestones.

*She was walking by ten months. Mine is already
using her spoon. This morning she tried to put on
her shirt.* They chat comfortably. I shift the pillows

propped around my daughter's floppy body. She falls
unable to hold the weight of her one-year-old world.
I grow accustomed to alarmed comments from strangers.

Her arms are flapping ready for take-off. She wears
a homemade weighted vest. Her shirt is wet with saliva.
Aren't you concerned they ask, as if I hadn't noticed.

I watch as other children snuggle and cuddle.
Mine arches her back away from me.
Her eyes wander. She cries to be put down.

Their mother love is met with smiles. Outstretched
arms . . . up up up. The attachment so intimate.
Mine's been tested. Stood against resistance

to my repeated insistence that she must try again,
and again. This devotion has no room for the depth
of despair, only determination.

There is nothing to be taken for granted.
This love must be unshakeable, unbreakable.
A bond not born, but built, with sparks flying

hammered into shape. This love the blue
flame of it—so hot with joy from small
wonders those other mothers will never know.

The Eighth Color of the Rainbow

At preschool, you draw a rainbow man
naming him Sadie-Eight.
You are sure he is hiding at home
behind the blinds. He is invisible
and invincible on the account of
no one can see him.

He is your nightmare.
He is all colors of the spectrum
and no colors at all.
Sometimes you can hear him tap dance
in between sparks and snaps
shaking the night sky.

After the storm
you can smell him hanging in the air.
He lingers between the colors,
leaving scratches of light
on your bedroom wall.
The local glass blower says

sometimes he sees him
outside the glory hole,
when the fire is too hot
and the mold too cold.
He creeps across the glass
leaving a chill-mark.

I know him as the sound
of a clock ticking,
sand seeping through the scrag,
the water dripping
down the back of my neck,
the shadow over my shoulder,

and the years gone by.

The Dance Teacher

There is a scratch in the vinyl record,
repeating repeating repeating—

Ms. Nina said hello!
Do you think Ms. Nina likes me?

What does Ms. Nina eat?
Does Ms. Nina have a boyfriend?

Ms. Nina is pretty!
What kind of car does Ms. Nina drive?

Ms. Nina was in our conversation
at breakfast, after school, and in our car trips . . .

I decide to talk about Brussels sprouts.
Brussels sprouts can be boiled,

steamed, stir fried, roasted and grilled.
Brussels sprouts are native to Belgium.

Brussels sprouts are in the cabbage family.
Brussels sprouts are rich in vitamin C and K.

Brussels sprouts are enhanced by butter,
bacon, mustard, pepper, and parmesan.

You are kicking the back of the driver's seat.
Mom, stop talking about Brussels sprouts!

I say o.k. I will just talk about BS;
BS grows on stalks, BS has a lot of dietary fiber,

BS goes by the scientific name gemmifera . . .
BS is a cruciferous, it is a cultivar.

Ms. Nina was your favorite.
Mine was BS. You were too small to understand.

You never mention Ms. Nina again.
I never speak about Brussels sprouts.

Postscript from my daughter.

You don't get it! Ms. Nina had everything.
She was Cinderella and all I wanted was her glass slipper.

Postcard—It's a Small, Small World

Just arrived to the character breakfast—the fuming Mad Hatter with his mercurous nitrate arrives at our table. The microscopic hairs in my daughter's organ of corti begin to vibrate wildly as my head is shaking no no no no. He is squeaking out his high-pitched lines . . .

Time is drowning, hearts are burning, heads are rolling, nothing can save you now, tick tock, tick tock.

We make the mad scramble to escape with a breakfast cookie from the hotel suite. Off to the rides. Stranded in the Matterhorn line for seven hundred six seconds, as we reach the front—tension soars. We proceed to the back of another line, thirty-six hundred seconds to Splash Mountain log jam. Just as our turn arrives, anxiety reappears. Over to another line . . . Pinocchio's daring journey. Too scary. Only half the day is gone . . . tick tock, tick tock. It's the thirty-foot clock rocking back and forth. On a flat facade is a smiling face . . . *it's a world of hope it's a world of fear.*

The Vacuum

With a flip of the switch
it performs a dervish,
dancing and spinning in circles
creating a suction so strong
that it shivers the skin.

The belt tightens
around the neck, the roller
spins and rubs against the rug.
You can smell the burning
as it swoops up static charges.

The dog startles and snarls.
My daughter hides in the closet.
Her legs are folded up.
Hands cover the tiny hairs
vibrating in her inner ears.

There are secret labyrinths
and spiral shadows swirling.
On the back of the closet door
an ancient symbol, a sigil
of storms yet to come.

Fishhooks

A woman with a split tongue provides desensitization training.
My daughter keeps demanding to touch her tongues.

The at-home treatment will cost four thousand dollars.
Follow the instructions. Put your daughter in a cardboard box.

Brush her skin every two hours for fourteen days.
Be religious. Never miss a brushing.

Sing—"this is the way we brush your skin,
brush your skin, brush your skin . . ." Say amen at the end.

Pretend it's a staycation. Smile. Follow brushing
with tapping the forehead then snap her fingers and toes.

Never question whether it works.
Swallow the fishhooks at the end of every sentence.

Try not to notice the bait . . . ask for a glass of water.
Make sure it is clear. Don't think about it.

Start tapping your own head. Write the check.
Go home and look at your tongue in the mirror.

Postcard—Staycation

The sizzle of sparklers and the bang snaps begin the Independence Day assaults. Windows rattle on each boom. There is no escape from black cats, m-80's, bottle rockets, poppers, ground spinners, snakes, roman candles, and firecrackers. I load my screaming toddler into her car seat with footie pajamas and deafeners, then drivedrivedrive until the night falls into the mountain hemlock. It is time to turn back. I carry her up to bed in the only room without windows. There I carefully place her on the floor next to the bathtub and cover her with a blanket. She remains there for days, eating and sleeping. It is the only safe place.

Just Get Over It

My sister calls and asks . . .
Isn't she over that yet?
As if autism is an infection invading
my daughter's immune system,
or a processing pathogen
causing brain congestion.
A temporary state of affairs
to be healed by chicken broth
and Vicks VapoRub. Something
you might sleep off, wait out,
wake up without.

Imagine that, I say, imagine
waking up and who you are
has disappeared.

The House of Barbini

Alfredo Barbini began learning the art of glass making in 1912, at age ten.
—20th century glass.com

During your fake-food phase
you begged to go to the expensive
furniture stores to examine bowls
of handcrafted purple grapes and plums.

Tugging on my arm you dragged me
through tabletop displays.
We moved from dining room to dining room
of carefully arranged trays on buffets.

You stopped to pick up the fuzzy plastic peaches,
and admire the painted props of gala apples
lying alongside apricots and avocados.
You touched the curved hips of brown pears

Each singularly sensual to your eye,
like the glass fruit from the House of Barbini.
You crave what you cannot have:
a succulent slice of an almost perfect life

with eternally braided French bread,
a collection of craftsman Italian baguettes,
and the portrait of a forever family
with pretend smiles, and unbruised fruit.

Through the Looking Glass

Take care of the sense and the sounds will take care of themselves.
—Lewis Carroll

Afraid to go inside you stand on the front
porch peering through the picture window.
Inside, he is hanging from the living room
ceiling twirling by a rope.

His colors are not in the right order.
Yellow should not be next to purple.
Blue should not be next to orange.
It hurts your eyes.

There are seven days in a week.
There are seven deadly sins.
There are seven colors out of order.
They should be roygbiv.

You keep shouting—
His colors are all mixed up.
Yellow should never be next to violet.
Blue should never be next to orange.

No one is listening.

You become the announcer in an *I Spy* book.
I spy with my little eye a picture of a stick.
I spy a little girl with a scarf covering her eyes.
I spy someone spinning her around,
she is swinging the stick.
I spy the mask on another girl, and another girl.
It's birthday girl's turn. She is blindfolded.
I spy Rainbow Man spinning around, around,
she is hurting him. I hear girls chanting.

Hit him harder!
Hit him harder!

He breaks open and his
insides fall on the living room floor.
I spy the girls grabbing candy.
Rainbow Man is dead.

You are standing outside on the porch
face pressed against the glass.
There is water coming out of your eyes.
It is salty, and it doesn't make sense.

What About Me?

It's seven-thirty on a December morning.
I'm on the way to drop off my kindergartener
in the school "round about" when she asks . . . Mom,
have you died yet? I take a breath,
feel the seat belt snug around me . . .

Not that I'm aware of. The sun's not yet risen.
It's the blue hour. I'm barely awake as
as I try and avoid potholes. Breast cancer
surgery fades in the rear view. She needs
certainty. So do I. Did they get it all?

The tattoo on my chest, a reminder
of six weeks of radiation. Then with a small
voice she continues . . . Well, what about me,
have I died yet? I adjust the rear-view mirror,
blink to make sure—*Nope, I can see you're still alive.*

Okay, good. But when I die, where will you
bury me? I try and focus, look both ways
before making the turn into the school lot.
*Mmmm, well, for sure it will need to be
somewhere beautiful.* Yay! she shouts.

Then bury me under the Christmas lights.

Postcard—What's the Difference

It's summer. We are on Ski to Sky Highway. Six of us in a vacation van with legs around luggage. Just outside of Squamish, on the curvy road, my niece loses her lunch. Everyone shows compassion. *So sorry. It will be ok. Would you like some water? Oh, that is so hard honey.*

The stench gets stuck in my daughter's seven-year-old sensory system. She can't stop talking about the sour smell. Someone in the family shouts *shut up, I said, shut up.* No one is sympathetic to her spouting the specific details of a spewed-up sandwich. She struggles to subdue the impulse . . . it is how she relieves stress. I am sitting next to her, searching for a soothing substitute.

Suddenly, my mother insists—she needs a comfort station—that means, soon! She can't hold it any longer, it is an uncontrollable urge, no one tells her to shut up.

Song of the Paper Doll

You announce you want to be a paper doll
a paper doll made from intimate folds
intimate folds of colorful washi paper
colorful washi paper that fits together

together they make an origami house
an origami house with an origami woman
an origami woman who is standing still
standing still next to a small child

a small child who is reading a book
a book that she has read many times
many times she wanted to be understood
to be understood like a book

like a book full of origami people
people whose expressions are folded fixed
fixed in place by paper creases
creases that do not hurt inside

hurt inside like a small child
a small child who has just announced
announced that she wants to be
to be a paper doll when she grows up

when she grows up she will learn
will learn about the Golden Venture
the Golden Venture refugees from China
from China where they escaped

they escaped looking for a new country
a new country where they landed
where they landed in prison
in prison they had nothing to do

nothing to do but play with paper
with paper they folded and created
created three dimensional designs
designs that were sold

that were sold to stop the pain
to stop the pain hidden in the folds
hidden in the folds of dreams
dreams of being accepted

being accepted into the fold
into the folds of paper
of paper dolls that don't hurt
don't hurt the small children.

Postcard—Tigh-Na-Mara

Having a wonderful time?! My daughter is frantically trying to avoid tiny parasitic pea crabs. Those red neck toothpicks are crawling all over the beach searching for oysters. The sun is setting inside their translucent shells. You can see their red gonads and tiny pinchers on the back of your eyelids. Her pinchers are clinging to my neck as I'm scrambling over rocks to escape to higher ground. The local tourists have their eyes sewn open like dolls, staring at us. At bedtime she wonders out loud. Mom, what would happen if I slit your throat? I stay awake all night wondering if my gonads would turn red.

Putting the Broken Pieces Together

Tucking you into bed you ask,
what does it mean to be dead?
I tickle you and answer,
you wouldn't be able to laugh—

Dead means your body doesn't
work anymore. You persist.
Would my fingers still work? No.
How about my ears, could I still hear?

No. If I was dead could I still eat?
Dead means nothing works.
Okay, but could I still breathe?
But, what about my brain?

Would my heart still beat?
As the organ list grows longer,
I can hear the church choirs
singing *Be Not Afraid.*

You look around the room.
Is that chair dead?
Yes, it is the dead wood of an oak.
Does it hurt when I sit on it?

No. How long do oak trees live?
Some live to be 300 years old.
Your eyes wander again,
how about my desk, is it dead?

Yes, your desk is the dead wood
from a sugar maple.
How long does a sugar maple live?
Sometimes they survive

as long as 400 years old.
Then I want to be a sugar maple
instead of an oak. I tuck the covers
up under chin and kiss your forehead.

Will I die when I'm asleep?
No, your body is just resting.
Good night, I love you.
Wait, Mom . . . does love die?

Postcard—Oregon Oceanside

The front of the house is a facade of greying shake shingles hanging over a cliff on the Pacific Ocean. The homeowner's instructions warn of a possible slide. The note says not to worry about the second-floor porch pulling away from the house. It's propped up by two by fours that aren't attached to the bluff.

I sit at the kitchen table drinking coffee out of a Melmac cup and reading A.J. Jacobs' *A Year of Living the Bible, Literally.* I just finished the chapter about stoning prostitutes with pebbles and avoiding sitting in the chairs of menstruating women. I look over into the living room, it's a stage mostly empty—just a couch and an old television. The lighting is soft.

My first grader is flipping the channels until it lands on the weather. Mesmerized for hours searching for a sudden squall, a tropical storm, a high surf—clutching the remote in her hand ready to silence any sound of thunder. This is her Disneyland. This is her Cedar Point. This is her Six Flags. There are no lines, no fast passes, it doesn't cost extra. Sitting in front of the T.V. riding tornados, hurricanes, floods and screening for sneaker waves, she's been watching all week, hoping to see hail stones in between the wavy lines and visual distortions from ocean winds. The cathode-ray vacuum tube is scanning parallel lines. The pattern is fixed.

Framing the Question

It is August, we're sitting in the waiting room.
I search patterns in the vintage wallpaper for answers.
It's 83 degrees, my daughter is wearing a winter coat.
The tight stitch blocks the sound of growth plates
that push against long bones in her arms and legs.
She picks flowers off the plaster, pinches the air, giggles.

Inside the office, windows are framed in old burr walnut
designed to calm the fears of those who contemplate the ledge.
The psychiatrist asks—*Why do you think you are here?*
A fly buzzes on the glass pane . . . searching for escape.
She thinks perhaps that's a good idea. Her response, a quadrilateral
is a parallelogram with four right angles. I'm in 4th grade.

Is it hard for you to stay focused? The shapes and sounds
collide with his words. He smells like wood or maybe black coffee.
I think he asked something, not sure. *Does your mind wander
all over the place?* Always . . . just ask my Mom. She knows.
Somewhere a ringtone is playing "by the seaside." At home
we have a glass float on the bookshelf from Seaside, Oregon.

The death-watch beetles keep tapping . . . tapping . . . tapping
she can hear their heads boring against the knotty whorl.
Can't you hear them? Fingers cover her ear tunnels, fearful
of the insanity inside the crevices of any emerging adults.
After thirty minutes the psychiatrist asks if there are any questions.
My daughter wonders out loud, are you married? My mom is still
   single—

Behind My Back

I remember my sister murmuring
about my decision to become
a single mother. *Why would*
she want to do that at her age?
She is not domestic, lacks common
Sense . . . What is she thinking!

My boss an intelligent chemist
commented, *seriously, you know*
you can't give that baby back.
Later the whispers would change.
It was clear that this was
no ordinary child.

My daughter dominated family
functions, demanded attention
with confusing intrusions, inventive
disruptions, at once both brilliant
and baffling. Befitting perhaps
my own peculiar personality.

I have wondered over the years
if their conclusions were correct?
Was I ill-prepared for the performance?
Juggling a high-powered job
running in heels across campus
proudly parenting with jelly on my jacket?

Dirty diapers, dishes left behind,
a daughter dragged to each endeavor.
Would I choose differently knowing
how inadequate my mothering might be?
How many mistakes I would make?
Could someone else have been more capable,

careful, calmer—yes of course. I don't
claim otherwise, on the contrary. Surely,
they must wonder about the probability
of this imperfect parental pairing?
But oh, the miracle in this match.
I'm telling you—is something to behold.

Keeping Your Head Down

In the fifth grade your best friend files a formal complaint
claims you rubbed your chest against hers. Breasts.

The teacher thinks it is sexual. You are only ten
and confused. You haven't developed yet. Like her.

It is the year your grandmother dies, slowly, with morphine
lipstick. She has no ability to swallow. The silence.

You understand. At her bedside vowels lose consonants
form OO, releasing the air of the unspoken. Large eyes.

On the playground an older girl asks how to pronounce s h i t.
You sound it out. An incident report is sent home. For swearing.

A classmate blows up a lunch bag and pops it near your face.
He announces you are annoying, so annoying. Asshole.

At the change of classes you walk in the hallway head down.
Sometimes it is best not to see what is coming. Your way.

Reading the Signs

1.

I have a picture in my head.
My daughter is standing
on the stage
at Larrabee State Park
singing to the grass
and wooly sunflowers.
Her age still counted in months.

Her only diagnosis
being a child. She is two
singing to an audience of air.
Seagulls were riding
the vibration and rising up
on a small echo off the back
of the amphitheater wall.

The wheels on the bus
go round and round
round and round
round and round.
The wheels on the bus
go round and round
all through the town.

2.

This year she celebrated
her twenty-third birthday.
Now she rides the city buses
watching out the window
at other people's lives.
Listening to songs
other people sing.

She stays seated
with her head resting
on the glass.
The street signs
appear and disappear
one diagnosis at a time.
There are familiar messages.

Slow.
One Way
Road Closed
Not a Through Street
Do Not Enter
Stop.
Dead End.

Op Po Sites

Your favorite children's board book
was Sandra Boynton's *Opposites*.

You dragged Op po sites around the house
announcing; up/down, heavy/light, day/night.

You commanded the world into two sides
front/back, east/west, worst/best.

If I was yes, you were no.
If I was no, you were yes.

A diminutive duetto, just the two of us
child/parent, together/apart.

In your teenage years our mother/daughter picture
is taken back-to-back, leaning for and against each other.

The long and short of it is bittersweet . . .
here/gone, present/absent, fact/fiction.

Postcard—Cedar Point Park

An amusement park reunion of adopted Chinese friends, all of the parents head off as a group . . . except us. We watch as somewhere under the sky a yellow streak rolls up and spikes across in forty seconds of a wild wicked twister. Their hair raises up with sensational millennium force and disappears. Not to be seen until day's end.

The frontal gate is labeled with the prefix dis. It comes before the rest of the word. As in dis-similar, dis-comfort, dis-count, dis-order, dis-ability. We are descending into the nine concentric circles of Dante's divine comedy. Dis is Purgatoria.

Postcards with no path to heaven until the chant "asperges me, asperges me, asperges me" turns to "Aspergers me, Aspergers me, Aspergers me." Wherein you hear the poet proclaiming, *O human race, born to fly upward, wherefore at a little wind dost thou so fall?*[1]

---

[1] Dante Alighieri, *The Divine Comedy,* Canto XII, lines 95–96

The Photograph

> "In China, the color red not only serves to express joy,
> but also to ward off evil."
> —*Chinese Color Theory,* Tin Christopher Hang

A classmate calls you pancake face. You come home confused.
In playground tag you are constantly "it"—there is no truce.
It is time to return for a visit to your native China.

First stop, Chengdu crafts factory. Up narrow concrete stairs,
we find old women sitting on stools weaving strips of bamboo
on vases. There are no machines. They welcome the break.

I snapped. A picture remembers what you can't. Their faces.
That evening we eat at Qin Shan Zhai medicinal restaurant.
Vats of snakes are marinating in rice, a powerful display

of serpents soaked and steeped, poised to strike Stunned
in silence, their venom neutralized in an earthy brown liquid,
denatured, slightly sweet.

Wine is poured into a shot glass. I swallow hard.
The stinging slows on the way down. It is your best friends
who belittled you. It burns my throat for years.

I glance at the menu, then order tender ears—slices of moon
pinched and dipped in a black sky of sesame and soy sauce.
They taste familiar to you.

Mandarin tones wind up and down the waitress's voice.
A waterfall of sounds spilling out into the crowded street.
You are bumping into yourself everywhere.

In the morning, we stop at your *finding spot.*
There is a small corner store, the street sign says Renmin
—Peoples Road. Your people. Your China.

Your culture. Your body. The bus takes us to the Foundling.
Fewer infants fill the cribs. You beg to hold a baby girl
—want to take her home. She looks like you.

They place her in your arms. I take a step back.
Peering through the view finder—our eyes meet.
There is a flash. In the photograph, your eyes are red.

Postcard—Sichuan, Ten Years Later

Just started day three of the China tour. It is June 26th. The temperature is tightly stitched, our skin silky with summer heat. We are visiting the Chengdu Panda Preserve. They have dressed my daughter in a sanitary gown and gloves. A red panda is placed on her lap with a slice of gala apple. In the picture she is happy. It doesn't last. Next stop, the Wenshu Buddhist monastery. Outside the temple is a narrow alleyway crowded with beggars clutching whatever coins are offered. There are no wheelchairs. A makeshift wooden board carries a disabled man. It is a path full of pleading. I hurry us along. Inside the temple incense burns images into memories. For months I will be asked why I took her to the temple. There will be no memory of cuddling a firefox. No, that didn't happen. She will say, that must have been a different child. I will remember the eyebrows on the golden laughing Buddha, they were raised.

It's Not a Picnic

This 4th of July
goes on for days.

We video chat
from your clothes closet.

Your head brushes against
the blouses.

Shirts sway and swing
on hangers as your hair

tangles on buttons. Later
you will curl up in the corner.

Cover up with a blanket.
Keep the door closed.

The only light—a blue
filter with short wavelengths.

Lines cross your eyes.
Deafeners conceal AirPods.

Your voice is distorted,
muffled by familiar terror.

Empty shoes surround you.
The air is unbuckled.

Feeding the Beast

The pantry is piled with chips.
Lay's sour cream and chives,
Tim's jalapeno,
Calidad tortilla,
Miss Vickie's sea salt and vinegar
Doritos nacho cheese
Kettle backyard barbeque
Cheetos and Fritos.
Every day you come home from work
with new purchases.

You have made chips the main course.
Harvest tomato is your favorite.
Ruffles sour cream and bacon—
a must for breakfast.
Chinese rice crackers wrapped
in seaweed count as the vegetables.
Dishes disappear into your bedroom.
Behind closed doors
crumbs collect on the nightstand.
Foil wrappers shine under the lamp.

You are nibbling your way
in and out of darkness. Downstairs
I can't find the box of oatmeal
or the can of cashews.
They are buried beneath
bin-bin rice crackers and
jelly-stuffed marshmallows.
I am staring at half-eaten comfort food
salty and sweet
the taste of grief in every bite.

You Stop

taking the medication.
Suddenly you
are accomplishing
astonishing feats.
The fireplace is fixed.
Flat shoes ordered,
bedspread on the way,
dress picked up,
invitations finalized.
Hyper focused
you feel fantastic
fearless
faultless
flashes of brilliance
fade
just before
you bump into yourself
and blame
the furniture for your bruises.

I shut down.
Turn off my phone
and head to the back trails
of Lake Padden.
The path is muddy
from spring rain.
Every step slippery,
unsteady.

You call 18 times
in two hours. Urgent texts
—please call, call me.
Where are you?
Why won't you answer?

I tread carefully.
There is no escape
for either of us.

Trying to Make Sense

I discover dirty dishes in the kitchen sink.
Dried chicken and garlic—
Rice a Roni stuck to the sides
of the stainless steel undermount.

It is how I know you are home—
the dishwasher sits empty.
Bottles collect on the nightstand,
Candy wrappers, crumbs on the couch.

I mention the obvious.
You storm into my bedroom
certain it is criticism claiming
that I always push your buttons.

The mad hatter asks
How is a dishwasher
like a teenage argument?
They are both automatic.

Over Parenting

You accuse me of coddling you,
like an egg slowly turning up the heat,
always just enough for small bubbles
to rise from the bottom pushing tenderly

so as not to break the inside. If you meant
coaxing, I am willing to confess to persistent
persuasion; weekly chores, childhood charts,
treasure boxes full of beads and Franklin books.

If you meant choices—set the table
or clear it off. Clean the bathroom
or vacuum. Enroll in classes
or go to work. I will take the blame.

If you meant caring about condoms
and cursing
and catfishing
and cash flow
and curfews
I accept the criticism.

But if you meant you just wanted
me to fix the eggs so they break
just right with the middle
still runny. Those, those
are already on your plate.

Celebrating Everybody

On this Mother's Day,
I walked around the lake, alone.

At twenty-four you have decided
you don't want me as your mother.

A stranger passes me
calling out "Happy Mother's Day!"

I swallow his words. They get stuck.
A fishbone buried in his salutation.

I come home, fix Chinese Pot Stickers.
You rave about the food, it is your favorite.

I take it as a compliment.
After dinner you quickly ask to be excused

leaving dirty dishes behind.
I sit down with a glass of wine.

Just before midnight you post on Facebook,
to no one in particular, *Oh, yeah,*

Happy Mother's Day Everybody.
I am Everybody, are you Everybody too?

Then there is a whole country of us.
I chuckle and click the "like" button.

No Offense, But . . .

Who do I call if you die?
You ask in between my coughing.
I reply factually.
Call your Aunt Clare.

I don't have her number . . .
then just text your cousin.
Okay, that will work.
Don't worry, I'm not dying.

Yeah, but just in case.
What if she doesn't answer?
Just leave a message.
Should I tell her you're dead

or will you do that?
If I am dead—I won't
be able to tell her.
Oh, yeah, never mind—

I better make a plan
to delete your number.
I don't want to accidentally
butt dial a dead person.

Grief

You surprised me
with lotus roses ten
scarlet blossoms

I set them on
the kitchen table
in an oversized

vase with a
curled lip
I could see through

the water
in your eyes
welling

and still I said
you could not
stay

After you left
I cut off
the stems.

What Love Looks Like

It's a warm Saturday night at Smokey Point rest stop,
the 18-wheelers are lined up with their chicken lights on.
There are no lot lizards available, but behind the counter
are two retired Lutheran church volunteers
brewing coffee as penance assigned by their wives.

My daughter accepts a Tinder date for dinner,
when the bill comes he thinks she owes him
a back seat of something more than conversation.
Her refusal earns a "get out" on the sidewalk drop off.
I am squinting at the vibrating phone at 1:15 in the morning.

Her name appears across the screen to the
music of *by the seaside*. The first sound is the sobbing
of *All I can see is evergreen trees. I don't know where I am.
Please come get me!* Read me any signs you can find—
It says Smokey Point. Coat over pajamas, I stumble to the car

Saying . . . find someplace safe to wait. The disciples take her in.
I find her standing with them eating chocolate chip cookies.
There is silence in the car on the way back. Until in the dark,
a small voice speaks up—*Mom, I love you, you know that right?*
Tell me again, I say, tell me again.

Watermarks

I calmly asked you not to come and visit.
Words I thought a mother never said.
Yet every time I pass your childhood
dance pictures on the stairs.
I pause

at the ponytails pulled tight, the ballet buns
bobby pinned. I tell myself one step at a time,
I will learn the *changement* position
feet switching in mid-air.
I pause

At the landing by your open bedroom door.
I peek in at the paper scattered on the floor.
My unfinished poems, waiting for me
to pick them apart.
I pause

At the dresser, necklaces hang from hat hooks.
A Justin Bieber ticket is still tacked to the bulletin board.
We stood in line for hours to hear *One Less Lonely Girl,
Never Say Never.*
I pause

At the almost empty closet, our family albums left behind.
I find your graduation photo proofs overlaid with watermarks,
I wonder if the image at the abandoned railway station
portrays how you felt.
I pause

At the thought that these poses were still life
photographs, shells washed up after the storm
and captured in just the right light
broken beautifully.
I pause

Two Dashes of Bitter

The burgundy and blue
camp chairs
are facing each other
set up under
the portico where

I used to sit with my daughter
in the breeze—
way chewing the evening's
silences.
Her hair's red highlights

streaking the horizon,
mine shaded grey
overcast, pulled back—
wards into what
she calls Old-Fashioned

made by muddling
sugar and two dashes of bitter
with a jigger of bourbon
over ice. I savor the thin
slice of orange peel

and swallow what is left
of the sun. No longer visible.
The long bend of light
creates a shadow on
her empty chair.

Hanging On

Dresser drawers are empty
closet clothes-less.
From your childhood bedroom window
I spot an upside down
deflated happy face
dangling
from the upper branch of a poplar.
Its string clinging
to an almost leafless limb.
I watch it
unable to let go.

Postcard—The Vdara

It sounded like a good idea, until it wasn't. It made sense, until it didn't. College spring break—Vegas. Madame Tussauds, the Shark Reef Aquarium, shopping at Miracle Mile. The sidewalk slickened with cards from gum snapping porn slappers. Souped up sounds on the strip. Shirts saturated in smoke. There is no sidestepping. Sixty minutes in line for Shark Reef Aquarium. Near the front, a boy in a wheelchair is injured. He's screaming as his father ices his skin. The ticket taker is clicking his camera. Step forward, smile, flash, step forward . . . smile ka-chick, ka-chick. Too crowded, can't see, too short, too skinny, squeezed on all sides. Back in the hotel, my head hurts. My daughter's splenetic. Even my jacket is full of static. You read this and laugh. Think you have been there. Then I tell you, we aren't in Vegas. We are at home and you're inside her body.

The Vow

You tell me you don't want me
to walk you down the aisle.

I already have given you away
in small pieces.

Or maybe it was me
being given away

like amber depression glass,
buried in boxes of Quaker Oats,

or handed out at gas stations.
I can smell the giveaways.

Imperfections appear
near the surface, air bubbles

trapped inside. I have my own
faults, flaws, and mold marks.

Either way, no one owns you.
You must. You must take hold.

Give of yourself freely, ensure an
equal say on your wedding day.

My blessing will be a poem
at your side, as you take each step,

turn around, the words
will be written all over my face.

On Trying to Fit In

A foot folded
bent and broken
bound until
sheathed inside
a lotus shoe.

How he made you
beautiful by
making you small
enough to fit
into his world.

A marriage
embroidered
with the fear
of being alone
unmatchable.

You become
benumbed
hobbling around
your husband's
three inches of insults.

No longer
able to feel
the pain
of not being able
to walk away.

Wake Up—Wake Up—Wake Up

*Fearing for your life
you beg to wake up.*

An orange shaft of
morning rises

beneath
a waning moon,

its hollow holds
onto the darkness.

A Cooper's hawk hovers
over a northern flicker

his quills are ripped
from the bone.

Red shafted
flight feathers

fall onto the driveway.
I pick one up

and carefully
place it in your hair.

Stop Pretending

Peter, the neighbor's little
blond-haired brother
plays husband to be.
The veil, an old faded blanket,
is bobby pinned to the bride's
unbrushed hair. The bouquet
of yellow dandelions
droops.

Your divorce is final in February.

Dun dun da dun; dun dun da dun
the wedding processional
marches up the cracked pavement
to the steps.
The groom trips
on the small stoop,
tumbles into the dense
thorns of a rugosa rosebush.

He deserved what he got.

The porch is now
a pretend hospital,
the patient
covered by a torn blanket.
Bobby pins become
surgical instruments.
Tweezers squeeze out
sharp stems.

It never stops hurting.

It isn't how you imagined.
There is no fairy-tale
wedding, no honeymoon.
Forced to flee in fear
from a marriage
that lasted less
than a year. It ended
in a thorny dissolution.

The prick is still imbedded.

Postcard—Unsettling on the Coast

Two hundred eighty-four miles to the front desk of the Rivertide suites. A looong weekend. Unlocking the hotel room door, my adult daughter declares dibs on the big bedroom. It has a tile floor, master bath, tub jets, expansive sink, and walk-in closet and her own TV. A place to cocoon. It's a short stroll to the ocean. Instead, she insists we drive to Tillamook. I resist. She persists. Begs to go home. Wants to order a $400 Lyft. It is dusk, the darkest stage of transitions. The in between. The unsettled. Where pupils grow larger. The sun droops out of sight. Evening unspools. I flip on the overhead. Too bright. Feel for a dimmer to switch—the mood. I suggest we hoof it to Finn's Fish House. The air is cool. The moon a sliver rising over the roof and under my fingernails. The streetlights soothe the path. Seated, I order a drink. Okay booze—A *Ta Kill Ya Martini.* You get the picture. She chooses battered cod and chips. *It's good, Mom, one of the best ever.* Ah, yes, yes. Wahoo! Hoorah! Ooh, this moment, is sooo delicious.

For Give Ness Sake

You order a posy
with an orange ribbon
I untie the bundle
and let it fall open

inside a milk bottle.
A rose stem is bending
at the waist unable
to support its petals.

Its protective outer guards
are wilted purple.
There is a cardette sticking
up between the pompons

and peonies. On the note card,
three letters M o m. I look up
and see a single rosette,
its head drooping.

and it is beautiful.

You Pretend Not to Miss Me . . .

It's the dog you long to visit.
It's the long drives around the lake.
It's the turquoise bedroom walls.
It's an iced chai latte at the local café.
It's your box of designer erasers.

You pretend not to remember . . .

Our driveway tether ball games,
forts built from couch cushions,
Sunday evenings watching
Candid Camera, nights cuddling
with your favorite books in bed.

I pretend not to be your mother . . .

Stop searching for answers
to questions never asked,
stop making emergency back-up
plans for your return,
stop shopping for your favorite foods.

I quit reacting when your name pops
up on my iPhone. Force myself to ignore
the silence that swallows the emptiness
that follows. My fingers lift the lid
and search for the heart shaped eraser.

Taproot

I am kneeling on the gravel
pulling out musk thistle.

It's a bitter tonic. I bite down
on spiny leaves, taste their intimacy.

It's pointless. The seeds don't fall far
from the parent plant. Discouraged

I stand and stretch to put away tools.
Small stones leave skin impressions.

In the hallway, I pause at the picture,
of my daughter. I try not to notice my journal

lying open on the coffee table.
A number 2 pencil is missing the point.

I pick up an eraser and smudge the page
where the word sorry is written

over and over and over—until
it wears a hole in the page.

Searching for Answers

We order pork fried rice, crispy crab Rangoon,
sautéed shrimp and Chinese dumplings.

You eat very fast, pack up left-overs
for later, forego the fortune cookies.

I don't. I make a small pile of brown bows,
individually wrapped and creased.

At the kitchen table I crack them
open and slide the small slips of paper

out from the thirteen grams of vanilla
and sesame sugar coated calories.

A pile of crumbs collects on the tablecloth
I don't care about the broken pieces

falling off the edge landing right where
the dog can lick them off the floor.

I study each sentence, anxious to read it,
sorting the lines into stacks of save or toss.

Fate fixed and folded over, baked inside.
Waiting to be opened. The next strip is blank.

Bare, naked. In the silence, Confucius says
Everything has beauty, not everyone sees it.

Have It

I carry you against my chest
wearing a white t-shirt
declaring
"I'm so tough
I vacation in Detroit"

Grabbing my breast
you cry, "Have It! Have It"
You miss the birth mother
never met, I miss the milk
that never came.

You are sure I snatched you
From the streets of Jiujiang,
shouting
Have Her!!
Have Her!!

The truth is—I did want you
and still do want you
to know that I wanted you.

If I could choose anyone
to be my daughter
I would still shout
Have Her!!
Have Her!!

I'm so tough
I vacation as your mother.

About the Author

Eileen Coughlin's first published poem, "Unfinished," was printed in 1991 by South Ash Press. The title would later launch her return to poetry. A former vice president in higher education, she retired in order to come face to face with the unfinished business of writing. She completed an MFA degree in Creative Writing at Pacific University in January of 2021, launching her as either an old face with new lines, or a new face among old lines. Her more recent poems have been published in *Literary Mama, Door is a Jar, Awakenings Review, Better Than Starbucks,* and the Village Books anthology. She resides in Bellingham, Washington.

www.ingramcontent.com/pod-product-compliance
Lightning Source LLC
Chambersburg PA
CBHW030909170426
43193CB00009BA/791